D

BLUE-RINGED OCTOPUS
Small but Deadly

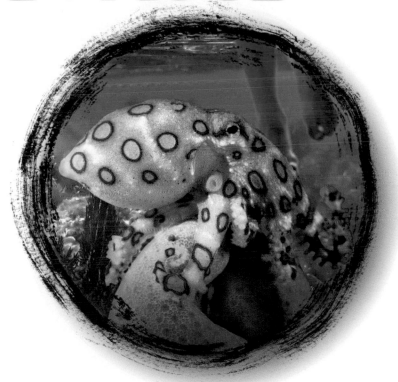

by Natalie Lunis

Consultant: Dr. Roy Caldwell
Professor of Integrative Biology
University of California, Berkeley

BEARPORT PUBLISHING

New York, New York

Credits

Cover and Title Page, © David Hall/Seaphotos.com; 4, © Dr. Roy L. Caldwell; 5, © Newspix/News Ltd/Bob Barker; 6, © Fancy Collection/SuperStock; 7, © Fred Bavendam/Minden Pictures; 8L, © David Hall/Seaphotos.com; 8R, © Dr. Roy L. Caldwell; 9, © Newspix/News Ltd/Bob Barker; 11, © Dr. Mark Norman; 12, © 2009 Marinethemes.com; 13T, © Dr. Mark Norman; 13B, © Mary Malloy; 14, © Doug Perrine/SeaPics.com; 15T, © 2009 marinethemes.com; 15B, © Maximilian Weinzierl/Alamy; 16, © Nat Sumanatemeya/imagequestmarine.com; 17, © John Lewis/Auscape; 18, © Lynn M. Stone/Nature Picture Library/Alamy; 19, © Nat Sumanatemeya/imagequestmarine.com; 20, © Dr. Mark Norman; 21, © Teresa Zubi/starfish.ch; 22T, © 2009 marinethemes.com; 22B, © 2009 marinethemes.com; 24, © Teresa Zubi/starfish.ch.

Publisher: Kenn Goin
Editorial Director: Adam Siegel
Creative Director: Spencer Brinker
Photo Researcher: Jennifer Bright
Design: Dawn Beard Creative

Library of Congress Cataloging-in-Publication Data

Lunis, Natalie.
  Blue-ringed octopus : small but deadly / by Natalie Lunis.
      p. cm. — (Afraid of the water)
  Includes bibliographical references and index.
  ISBN-13: 978-1-59716-944-8 (library binding)
  ISBN-10: 1-59716-944-7 (library binding)
  1. Blue-ringed octopuses—Juvenile literature. I. Title.

  QL430.3.O2L86 2010
  594'.56—dc22
                                    2009009334

For more information, write to Bearport Publishing Company, Inc., 101 Fifth Avenue, Suite 6R, New York, New York 10003. Printed in the United States of America.

10 9 8 7 6 5 4 3 2 1

Contents

Blue Means Danger.................................... 4

Keep Breathing!...................................... 6

Eight Arms, No Bones............................. 8

Hidden Homes.. 10

Cracking Crabs 12

Surrounded by Enemies....................... 14

A Disappearing Act 16

A Powerful Poison................................ 18

Do Not Disturb! 20

Other Deadly Sea Creatures.................... 22

Glossary 23

Index... 23

Bibliography.. 24

Read More... 24

Learn More Online.................................. 24

About the Author 24

Blue Means Danger

Anthony Cerasa was exploring the water's edge at Suttons Beach in Redcliffe, Australia. The curious three-year-old could see all kinds of rocks and shells in the **shallow** ocean water. He even saw a tiny octopus—so small it was about the size of a child's hand.

Anthony picked up the little brown creature. As he held it, something surprising happened. Bright blue lines and rings appeared on its skin. The boy didn't know it, but the blue markings meant danger. The little creature was a blue-ringed octopus—the only kind of octopus that is known to be deadly to people. Its change in color was a sign that it was about to bite.

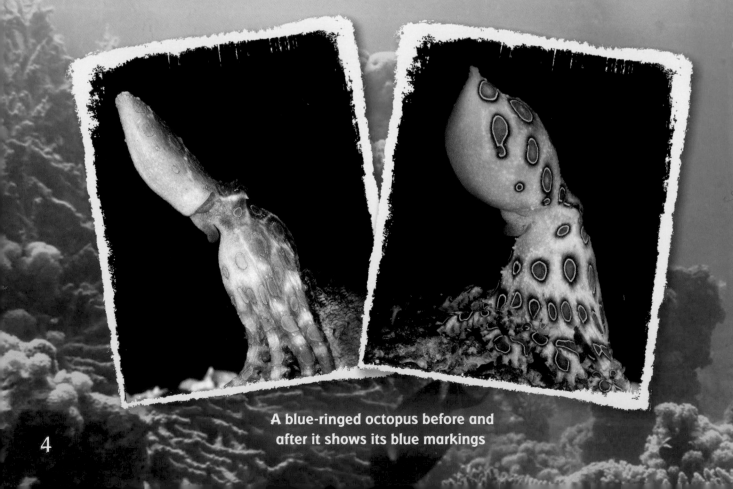

A blue-ringed octopus before and
after it shows its blue markings

Almost all blue-ringed octopus bites happen when children or other beachgoers pick up the tiny creatures.

Keep Breathing!

The blue-ringed octopus in Anthony's hand was so small that he didn't even feel the bite. He put the little creature back in the water after showing it to his mother. A few minutes later, however, he started feeling strange. He told his mother that his legs felt "floppy" and that he couldn't walk.

Luckily, Anthony's mother acted quickly. If she hadn't, her son would soon have been unable to breathe. She made sure he was rushed to a nearby hospital. From there, doctors sent him to a larger hospital where he was put on a **respirator**. After breathing with the help of the machine all night, he was safe. The **venom** he had received from the bite had stopped working. Anthony was back to being a healthy three-year-old.

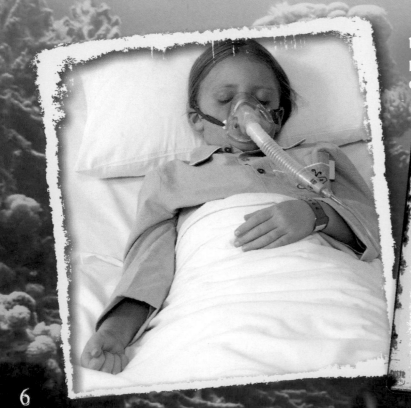

Respirators like this one help people with serious illnesses or injuries breathe.

DANGER

When a blue-ringed octopus bites a person, it sends venom into its victim's body. The venom makes the person feel weak at first. Then it makes him or her unable to breathe.

Hidden Homes

Octopuses, no matter how big or small, are shy creatures. They spend most of their time in a hidden home called a **lair**. This secret hiding place might be a crack in a rock, or it might be a cave-like opening in a pile of rocks.

Because the octopus's body is boneless and rubbery, it can squeeze into a very small space. Sometimes a little blue-ringed octopus will even turn an empty seashell or an empty can into a lair. While it is curled up inside, it doesn't just rest or sleep, however. Usually, it keeps an eye on the outside world—watching for enemies and for tasty treats that might be passing by.

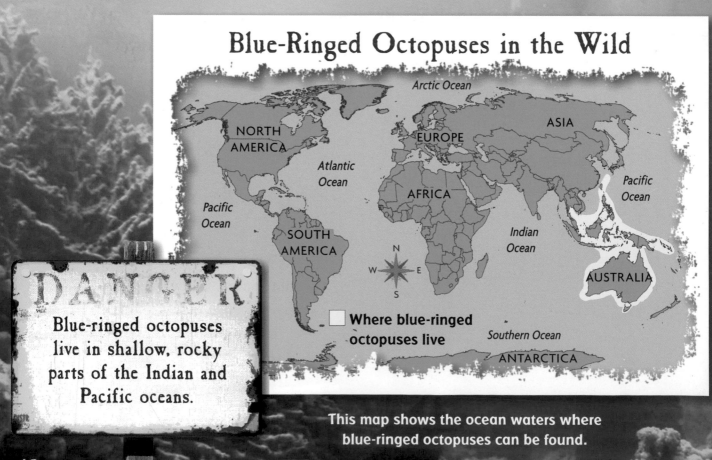

Blue-Ringed Octopuses in the Wild

Arctic Ocean

NORTH AMERICA

EUROPE

ASIA

Atlantic Ocean

Pacific Ocean

AFRICA

Pacific Ocean

SOUTH AMERICA

Indian Ocean

AUSTRALIA

☐ **Where blue-ringed octopuses live**

Southern Ocean

ANTARCTICA

DANGER

Blue-ringed octopuses live in shallow, rocky parts of the Indian and Pacific oceans.

This map shows the ocean waters where blue-ringed octopuses can be found.

A blue-ringed octopus
using a shell as a lair

Cracking Crabs

Sometimes a blue-ringed octopus needs to leave its lair. The main reason it goes out is to look for food. To get around, it can use its arms to walk along the ocean floor. It can also swim by pumping water out of a tube on its body called a **siphon**.

Crabs are the little octopus's favorite food. To catch one, the octopus grabs it with its arms, using its suckers to hold on. Then it brings the victim to its mouth. The mouth has a strong, bird-like beak, which the octopus uses to bite into the crab. As it does, venom enters the crab's body and **paralyzes** it. Now that the crab cannot move or struggle, the octopus can go on biting into it and eating the soft meat inside.

blue-ringed octopus

crab

Blue-ringed octopuses like to eat crabs, as well as shrimp and fish.

A blue-ringed
octopus swimming

siphon

mouth

A view of a blue-ringed
octopus from below

DANGER

An octopus's mouth and
beak are on the underside
of its body, in the
middle of its eight arms.

Surrounded by Enemies

The shallow part of the ocean where the blue-ringed octopus lives and hunts is a dangerous place. It is full of sharks and other fish that kill and eat octopuses. One of these hungry fish, the moray eel, hides out in a rocky lair of its own, waiting for **prey** to swim by. When it sees something good to eat, it pops out and tries to grab the animal in its teeth.

Luckily, a blue-ringed octopus is far from helpless. It has a weapon it can use against attackers—its deadly bite. Before it uses its venom, however, the eight-armed creature tries some surprising tricks. Often they help it escape trouble before it happens.

A moray eel in its lair

DANGER

Blue-ringed octopuses and moray eels often live in **coral reefs**. These rock-like underwater structures are home to a huge variety of sea creatures.

Large crabs like this one sometimes eat blue-ringed octopuses.

Triggerfish also live in coral reefs and hunt blue-ringed octopuses.

A Disappearing Act

Any octopus, including the blue-ringed octopus, would rather swim away from danger than fight. However, an octopus can do more than make a quick getaway. It can also make a quick color change.

Most of the time, the octopus changes color in order to blend in with its surroundings. In less than a second, it can take on the color of the brown, sandy ocean floor or a red coral reef. Often, this trick helps it hide from enemies. If it fails to work, however, the blue-ringed octopus shows its bright blue markings. At that point, an enemy may pay attention to the warning and go away. Otherwise, it will receive a deadly bite from the little octopus's razor-sharp beak.

This blue-ringed octopus hides by making the color of its body match the sandy ocean floor.

DANGER

An octopus doesn't just change its color. It can also make its skin bumpy to match the texture of its surroundings.

In order to hide, this blue-ringed octopus has made its skin look like the rocky sand around it.

A Powerful Poison

Blue-ringed octopuses do not seek out humans. They just want to be left alone. When the little creatures are out hunting for food, however, they sometimes meet up with people. Once in a while, the meeting ends with a dangerous bite. Why? A blue-ringed octopus may feel the need to defend itself when a person tries to pick it up out of curiosity or steps on it by accident.

Even though someone who has been bitten may not feel the actual bite, the poison starts acting quickly. First the victim feels weak. Blurry vision and trouble speaking and swallowing often come next. Then the victim may become paralyzed and be unable to breathe. At that point, death can occur—unless rescuers act quickly.

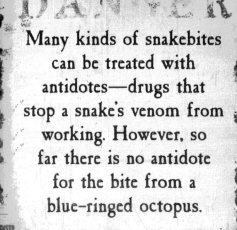

DANGER

Many kinds of snakebites can be treated with antidotes—drugs that stop a snake's venom from working. However, so far there is no antidote for the bite from a blue-ringed octopus.

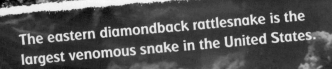

The eastern diamondback rattlesnake is the largest venomous snake in the United States.

One blue-ringed octopus has enough venom to kill about ten people. Its venom is more powerful than the venom found in any snake, spider, or other land animal.

Do Not Disturb!

A blue-ringed octopus's venom can quickly kill a person, but is the little creature a big danger to humans? Fortunately, there have been only a few known deaths from its bite. While several people are bitten each year, most recover thanks to quick action from rescuers. For example, victims are sometimes given **mouth-to-mouth resuscitation** until they can be rushed to a hospital for more help with breathing.

There's even more good news for people who visit the beaches where the **lethal** little sea creatures are found. Namely, there's a simple way to avoid a deadly bite. If you see a tiny octopus, leave it alone. Do not pick it up and wait to see if it flashes a blue warning. By the time you do, it's probably too late!

In Australia, some beaches put up signs to warn people about blue-ringed octopuses.

DANGER

Some people who have survived a blue-ringed octopus's bite have told about a strange experience. Rescuers and others around them thought they were dead. The victims, however, were aware of everything that was going on—but were unable to move or speak!

There's only one safe way to see a blue-ringed octopus showing its blue markings — in photos!

Other Deadly Sea Creatures

**The blue-ringed octopus is one of the most deadly of all sea creatures.
Here are two more sea creatures that can kill with poison.**

Pufferfish

- Some kinds of pufferfish have the same kind of poison in their bodies as the blue-ringed octopus. If eaten, the poison can paralyze a person and stop his or her breathing.
- In Japan, pufferfish is considered a treat to eat. Highly trained chefs remove the poisonous parts before serving it.
- Sometimes some of the poison remains in the fish dish, however. About 100 people per year die as a result of eating it—far more than are killed by the bite of a blue-ringed octopus!

Cone Shells

- Cone shells are sea snails. Some kinds have venom that is similar to that of the blue-ringed octopus.
- The venom paralyzes the small sea creatures that the cone shells catch and eat. The cone shells inject the venom using their teeth.
- Sometimes people are stung when they pick up venomous cone shells. The worst stings can cause death.

Glossary

coral reefs (KOR-uhl REEFS) groups of rock-like structures formed from the skeletons of sea animals called coral polyps; usually found in shallow tropical waters

lair (LAIR) the underwater home of an octopus, moray eel, or other sea creature that needs to stay hidden

lethal (LEE-thuhl) able to kill

mollusks (MOL-uhsks) a group of animals, including snails, clams, oysters, and octopuses, that have no bones but may have hard shells

mouth-to-mouth resuscitation (MOUTH-too-*mouth* ri-*suhss*-i TAY-shuhn) a type of rescue in which someone breathes into the mouth of another person in order to get oxygen to his or her brain

paralyzes (PA-ruh-*lize*-iz) to cause something to be unable to move

prey (PRAY) animals that are hunted and eaten by other animals

respirator (RESS-puh-*ray*-tur) a machine used in a hospital to help a person breathe

shallow (SHAL-oh) not deep

siphon (SYE-fuhn) a tube-shaped part of an octopus's body that is used to let out water

suckers (SUHK-urz) cup-shaped bumps on an octopus's arms that help the octopus hold on to rocks, food, and other objects

venom (VEN-uhm) poison that some animals can send into the bodies of other animals through a bite or sting

Index

arms 8–9, 12–13, 14
Australia 4, 10, 20
beak 12–13, 16
Cerasa, Anthony 4, 6
changing colors 4, 16–17
cone shells 22
coral reefs 14–15, 16
crabs 12, 15
enemies 10, 14–15, 16

food 12, 18
habitat 10
lair 10–11, 12, 14
mollusks 8
moray eel 14
mouth 12–13
mouth-to-mouth
   resuscitation 20
pufferfish 22

rescuers 18, 20
respirator 6
siphon 12–13
size 8–9
suckers 8, 12
venom 6, 12, 14, 18–19, 20, 22
weight 5

Bibliography

Caldwell, Dr. Roy. "What Makes Blue-Rings So Deadly?" *The Cephalopod Page.* www.thecephalopodpage.org/bluering2.php

Cerullo, Mary M. *The Octopus: Phantom of the Sea.* New York: Dutton (1997).

Desmond, Rosemary. "Boy Survives Octopus Bite," *The Australian* (October 9, 2006). www.theaustralian.news.com.au/story/0,20867,20549146-5006786,00.html

http://marinebio.org/species.asp?id=403

Read More

Cerullo, Mary M. *The Truth About Dangerous Sea Creatures.* San Francisco: Chronicle Books (2003).

Gross, Miriam J. *The Octopus.* New York: Rosen (2006).

Spirn, Michele. *Octopuses (Smart Animals).* New York: Bearport (2007).

Learn More Online

To learn more about the blue-ringed octopus, visit
www.bearportpublishing.com/AfraidoftheWater

About the Author

Natalie Lunis has written many science and nature books for children. She lives in the Hudson River Valley, just north of New York City.